Jesus Loves the Little Children

Treasury of Poems, Prayers, and Promises

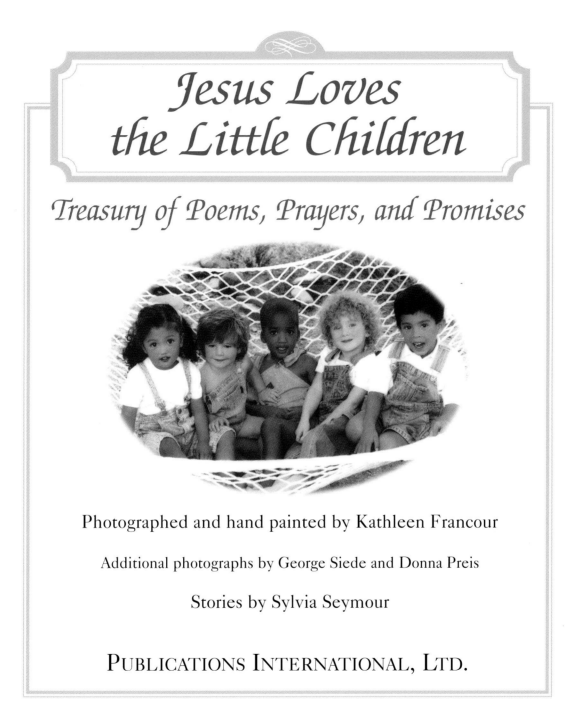

Photographed and hand painted by Kathleen Francour

Additional photographs by George Siede and Donna Preis

Stories by Sylvia Seymour

PUBLICATIONS INTERNATIONAL, LTD.

Louis Weber, C.E.O.
Publications International, Ltd.
7373 North Cicero Avenue
Lincolnwood, Illinois 60646

ISBN: 0-7853-1836-4

Table of Contents

Jesus loves every child.
And through His example,
children can learn to live,
and love, and grow.

Good Morning, God

Each new day brings
the love of God.

A Surprise for Mommy

"I'll surprise Mommy this morning!" Johnny whispered happily. "I'm a big boy and I can get dressed by myself." He stepped into his shorts and wiggled his head and arms through his pullover shirt. It was a little bit crooked, but the tag was in the back just like Mom said it should be.

Johnny pulled on his socks. "Now, which shoe?" he thought. "Jesus will help me. He always helps me when I ask Him."

Johnny closed his eyes and prayed. "Dear Jesus, please help me find the right shoe." He put his foot into his shoe. It fit! The other shoe was a perfect fit, too.

"Look Mommy," called Johnny. "I did it! I did it!"

I'll Be a Sunbeam

Jesus wants me for a sunbeam
　　To shine for Him each day.
In every way try to please Him
　　At home, at school, at play.

A sunbeam, a sunbeam,
　　Jesus wants me for a sunbeam.
A sunbeam, a sunbeam,
　　I'll be a sunbeam for Him.

Lord Jesus Christ, be with me today,
  And help me in all I think, and do, and say.

O God, Creator of Light,
At the rising of Your sun this morning,
let the greatest of all light, Your love,
rise like the sun within our hearts.
                    Amen.

Rise and Shine

Lucy did not want to get up. It was too early. Why couldn't she sleep a little longer? She dragged herself out of bed and stood looking out of her window. The sun was like a tiny face peeking over the treetops.

"Hello, Sun," Lucy said, yawning. "Do you hate to wake up, too?"

The sun was bigger now, spreading its light across the sky like a gentle smile.

"Lucy," Mother called, "breakfast is ready."

Lucy stretched sleepily and thought about the tasty breakfast waiting for her downstairs. She smiled at the happy sun and whispered, "Thank you, Jesus, for the morning sun. And thank you for this new day."

When Morning Gilds the Skies

When morning gilds the skies,
    My heart awaking cries:
May Jesus Christ be praised!
    Alike at work and prayer
To Jesus I repair:
    May Jesus Christ be praised!

Does sadness fill my mind?
    A solace here I find:
May Jesus Christ be praised!
    Or fades my earthly bliss?
My comfort still is this:
    May Jesus Christ be praised!

I am small,
my heart is clean;
let no one dwell in it
except God alone.
Amen.

This morning, God,
this is Your day.
I am Your child.
Show me Your way.
Amen.

God's Alarm Clock

"Cock-a-doodle-do," crowed the rooster from the barnyard fence. Luke stretched his arms over his head and yawned.

"Time to get up," Luke said to himself, stretching again. "Rooster always knows when it is morning." He could hear his parents moving about in the kitchen. They heard the rooster, too. Soon the smells of breakfast floated up to Luke's room. "I love living on a farm."

"Mom," said Luke at breakfast. "How does Rooster always know when to wake us up?"

"He just knows," Mother said, smiling. "Roosters are God's alarm clocks."

For this new morning and its light,
    For rest and shelter of the night,
For health and food, for love and friends,
    For every gift Your goodness sends,
We thank You, gracious Lord.

This is the day which the Lord has made;
let us rejoice and be glad in it.

Psalm 118:24

Hark! A Herald Voice Is Calling

Hark! a herald voice is calling,
    Christ is nigh, it seems to say;
"Cast away the dreams of darkness,
    O ye children of the day!"

Wakened by the solemn warning,
    Let the earth-bound soul arise;
Christ, her Sun, all sloth dispelling,
    Shines upon the morning skies.

The First Day of School

When Robert saw the big school building and all the children, he whispered to his mother, "Do I have to go?"

"Yes, Robert," Mother said softly as she put her arms around him. "I know that you are nervous about your first day at school. Let's pray to Jesus to look out for you today." Mother and Robert prayed that he would not be lonely or scared at school. They walked through the school's big front door. When they reached his classroom, he heard a friendly voice.

"Hi, Robert," Scott called.

Robert's face broke into a smile when he saw his friend. "Are you in this class, too?" He wasn't afraid anymore. God had sent him a friend.

The year's at the spring
　　And day's at the morn;
Morning's at seven;
　　The hillside's dew-pearl'd;
The lark's on the wing;
　　The snail's on the thorn;
God's in His heaven—
　　All is right with the world.

Robert Browning

Good morning, Lord!
Be with me all day long,
until the shadows lengthen,
and the evening comes,
and the hustle and bustle of life is done,
and those at work are back at home.
Then in Thy mercy, grant us safe lodging,
and a Holy rest, and peace at the last.
                              Amen.

Lord, teach us to pray.

The Right Side of the Bed

Leah and Joanna are sisters. One morning Joanna woke up as cross as a bear. Leah couldn't go back to sleep because Joanna was fussing and complaining.

Dad heard the noise and stuck his head into the room. "What's going on in here?"

"Daddy," groaned Leah, "Joanna won't let me go back to sleep."

"Go back to sleep!" snapped Joanna crossly. "I don't care what you do!"

"Wait a minute, Joanna," grinned Dad. "It isn't nice to snap at your sister like that. I think you must have gotten up on the wrong side of the bed this morning."

Joanna looked puzzled. "But Daddy," she asked, "how do you know which is the 'right' side?"

"The 'wrong' side just means that you are grumpy, not cheerful and kind as you should be," explained Dad. "Now apologize to your sister for yelling."

"I'm sorry, Leah. I will try to find the 'right' side of the bed before waking up from now on."

Rise and Shine

Rise and shine and give God the glory, glory!
Rise and shine and give God the glory, glory!
Rise and shine and give God the glory, glory,
　　Children of the Lord!

The Lord is all I need.
He takes care of me.

Psalm 16:5

I have a busy day today, Jesus.
Help me to do my chores with cheer
and be kind to others,
even if they are not kind to me.
Watch over me as I walk the dog
and play with my friends.
Lord, I have a busy day.
Thank you for being by my side.

Amen.

Is the Sun Sleeping Today?

Nicole peeked out of her bedroom window. It was morning, but the sky was dark and dreary. Nicole pulled the covers up over her head and tried to go back to sleep.

"Nicole, it's time to get up," called Mother.

"The sun is sleeping today," yawned Nicole. "I think I want to sleep, too."

"Come on, Nicole. It's time for you to get up. You know, cloudy days have their good points, too."

"What's one good thing about cloudy days?"

Mother thought for a moment. "Well, if God made every day sunny, we might forget to appreciate the sun."

How Brightly Beams the Morning Star!

How brightly beams the morning star!
   What sudden radiance from afar
Doth glad us with its shining?
   Brightness of God, that breaks our night
And fills the darkened souls with light
   Who long for truth were pining!
Newly, truly, God's word feeds us,
   Rightly leads us,
Life bestowing.
   Praise, O praise such love overflowing!

Dear Father,

As we start this day, please guide us.

Please help Mom and Dad as they work.

Please help me at school.

Please help my little sister at home,

and all my other friends and family.

Amen.

Bless My Family

A family is God's way
of surrounding us with love.

Daddy's Hat

"Hi, Daddy! Look at me!" giggled three-year-old Leo. His eyes and ears were hidden by a big brown hat. Only his mouth, still laughing, could be seen on his tiny face. "My hat!" said Leo as his plump little hands clutched the cherished hat.

"Actually, it's my hat, son," Father said gently. "It will be a while before it will fit your head. Even Baby Jesus had to grow bigger in order to do the job that God planned for Him. God wants you to be yourself the way you are, but I guess you may wear the hat for now!"

I sought my soul,
   But my soul I could not see.
I sought my God,
   But my God eluded me.
I sought my brother,
   And found all three.

I know that as I grow bigger
my love for my mother and father
will grow bigger, too.
Thank you, Jesus, for my parents.

A Real Family

"One, two, three, four, five, six," Jason counted the people in the book that he was reading. "This family has six people."

"That's a big family," said Mother.

"One, two, three, four, five. That's another big family."

Dad was reading the newspaper, but he stopped and motioned to Jason to come sit on his lap.

"Dad," asked Jason, "why don't we have a big family? There are only three of us. Are we a real family?"

"Jason," said Dad, "it doesn't matter how many people are in a family. It's the love that the family has for each other that makes it a real family."

Honor your father and your mother.

Exodus 20:1

Sing to God, sing praise to His name,
   extol Him who rides on the clouds—
His name is the Lord—
   and rejoice before Him.
A father to the fatherless, a defender
   of widows, is God in His holy dwelling.

Psalm 68:4-5

Sharing with Little Sister

Kimberly and Daniel both wanted the ball. "Give it to me!" screamed Daniel. "It's my ball!"

"You have to share. Mom said so. It's my turn!"

"I want it! It's mine!"

Daddy heard the children arguing. "I think you'd better both go outside and come back when you decide that you can get along. I'll keep the ball until you get back."

"It isn't much fun to be outside without the ball," Daniel complained.

"Let's ask Dad to let us both have the ball. We can play catch together."

"Yes, we can share it! It's more fun if we share."

Peace be to this house
and to all who dwell in it.
Peace be to them that enter
and to them that depart.

Dear Lord,
Please be sure that my family
knows that I love them very much,
even during the times I don't show it.

Amen.

Who Wants to Play with a Sister

"Mommy, why can't Billy and Tommy come over?" whined Daniel. "I want to play with them. They are my best friends."

"Why don't you play with Kimberly?"

"Kimberly's my sister! Who wants to play with a little sister!"

Kimberly came into the room carrying two cowboy hats. "Hi, Daniel. Let's play cowboy. I have some hats. We can use broomsticks for horses."

The children asked their mom for two brooms. "Yahoo!" cheered Kimberly.

"Let's go outside and ride our horses," said Daniel.

"Good idea, big brother," said Kimberly.

"Hey, this is fun! I'm glad you're my sister."

Lord Jesus,
Please take care of my family.
Keep them healthy and safe from harm.
I love them very much.

                    Amen.

Dear Jesus,
My parents work very hard
to bring me the things I need.
Please help me to be good
so that their lives are a little easier.
Thank you, Lord.

                    Amen.

Family Pictures

Matthew looked at the picture he had drawn of Mommy, Daddy, brother Aaron, baby Lauren, and Whiskers.

"It doesn't look right. No one looks right. I just can't draw." Tears trickled down Matthew's cheeks. He wanted to tear up the picture and throw it away.

"Let me see your picture," said Aaron. He looked carefully at the picture his brother had made.

"Why this is beautiful, Matthew. I like the way you put a smile on each of our faces. Jesus likes children's pictures the best, especially pictures of happy faces."

Then Matthew smiled!

Here on my bed my limbs I lay,
 God grant me grace my prayers to say:
O God! preserve my mother dear
 In strength and health for many a year;
And, O preserve my father, too,
 And may I pay him reverence due;
And may I my best thoughts employ
 To be my parents' hope and joy;
And, O preserve my brothers both
 From evil doings and from sloth,
And may we always love each other,
 Our friends, our father, and our mother:
And still, O Lord, to me impart
 An innocent and grateful heart,
That after my great sleep I may
 Awake to Thy eternal day! Amen.

Samuel Taylor Coleridge

Baby Brother

Kim looked at the tiny baby in her mother's arms. His face and arms seemed fragile peeking out of the blanket.

"Would you like to hold him?" Mother asked.

"But, Mom, he's so small!"

"You are a big sister now, Kim." Mother handed the tiny bundle to her daughter. "You can ask Jesus to help you. Jesus loves little children. Here, just hold the baby gently."

Kim felt the wiggly little baby in her arms. She closed her eyes and prayed softly, "Please Jesus, keep my little brother safe. Help me to be a good big sister to him."

Thank you, Lord Jesus,
for my brothers and sisters.
Without them, our house
would be too quiet.

Dear Jesus,
My brother and I may
sometimes fight, but I know
that he loves me and I love him.
Please know, Lord Jesus,
that we love You, too.

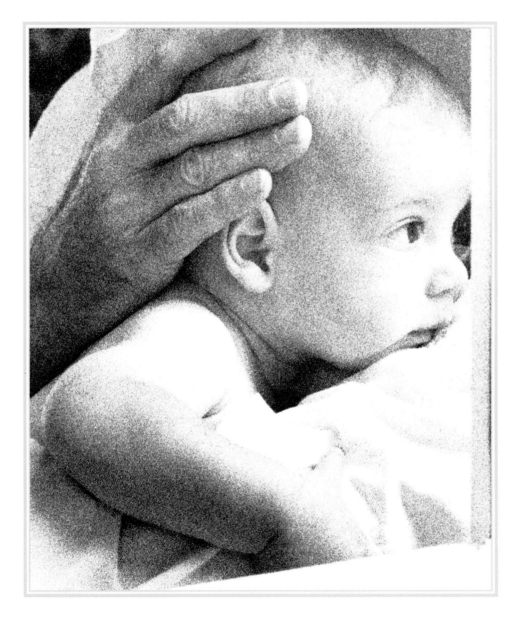

Dear Lord,

Thank you for my grandparents.

They always have time to read to me

or play games.

They like to tickle and play and laugh.

And they like ice cream

and going to the park, too.

Mostly though, God, they love me.

Please take care of them, Lord,

I think they must be a lot like You.

Dear Jesus,
Thank you for my sister.
She likes to play the same
games as I do. She likes to
climb our favorite tree and
she takes turns on the swing—
sometimes letting me swing longer!
She is the best sister in the world.
Thank you, Jesus, for my sister.

Amen.

Dear Jesus,
Funny how my brother looks
just like me. At night we pray
together, so don't think it is
me praying twice.

                    Amen.

I see myself when I look at
my brother. Thank you, Jesus,
for giving me my own special mirror.

God bless all those that I love.

God bless all those that love me.

God bless all those that love those that I love,

And all those that love those who love me.

Bless This Food

A blessing at mealtime is the perfect
way to say, "Thank you, God."

I Want to Help, Too

Maria loved to follow her mother around the kitchen. Mother was the best cook in the world! "Can I help?" Maria asked. Mother was very busy. Company was coming for dinner tonight.

"Please, Mommy, I want to cook, too," Maria begged. Mother looked at her daughter. "Yes, Maria, I have just the job for you. Let's get a step stool so you can reach the counter. I really need you to stir the cake for me. It is a very special dessert for our friends."

Maria hummed as she stirred.

"What a fine job you did on the cake," said Mother. "Now you may lick the spoon."

O You who feeds the little bird,
bless our food, O Lord.

Let us in peace eat the food
that God has provided for us.
Praise be to God for all His gifts.

      Amen.

O God, make us able
for all that's on the table!

      Amen.

We thank Thee, Lord,
   For happy hearts,
For rain and sunny weather;
   We thank Thee, Lord,
For this our food,
   And that we are together.

God is great,
   God is good,
And we thank Him
   For our food.
Amen.

Two Spoons

"Mommy, may Sarah eat with us tonight? Her mom is working late. Please, Mommy, please!" begged Michelle.

Mother looked at little Sarah. She looked so lonely. "Yes, Sarah may stay."

The dinner was delicious. Michelle helped her mother clear the table for dessert. They were having her favorite dessert, chocolate pudding. Suddenly Michelle realized that there wasn't a bowl for Sarah. What should she do? She gave the last bowl to her best friend.

Sarah saw that Michelle did not have any pudding. "Oh, Michelle," she said. "This is too much pudding for me. Can we share?"

Michelle's face lit up with joy. "Yes, Sarah. I'll get two spoons."

We Gather Together

We gather together to ask the
Lord's blessing,
He chastens and hastens
His will to make known.
The wicked oppressing now
cease from distressing,
Sing praises to His name,
He forgets not His own.

Our Garden

The Lee family was eating food from their garden for supper. Gregory was proud of the golden ears of corn that he helped grow. Richard beamed as Mother placed the potatoes he grew on the table. Jane's onions were in the salad with Mom's cucumbers and Dad's tomatoes.

"These are *my* potatoes and I want them all," Richard announced as he pulled them over to his plate.

"Well, then you can't have any of *my* corn," said Gregory.

"Are you forgetting who made all the vegetables?" asked Mother.

"We did!"

"God made them and we just took care of the garden. Now let's all share and thank God for the food He has given us."

Bless Thou the Gifts

Bless Thou the gifts our hands have brought;
    Bless Thou the work our hearts have planned.
Ours is the faith, the will, the thought;
    The rest, O God, is in Thy hand.
Amen.

Come, Lord Jesus,
    Be our guest.
Let these gifts
    To us be blessed.

Now Thank We All Our God

Now thank we all our God,
     With heart and hands and voices,
Who wondrous things hath done,
     In whom His world rejoices;
Who from our mothers' arms
     Hath blessed us on our way
With countless gifts of love,
     And still is ours today.

O may this bounteous God
     Through all our life be near us,
With ever joyful hearts,
     And blessed peace to cheer us,
And keep us in His grace
     And guide us when perplexed,
And free us from all ills,
     In this world and the next.

Thank You for Green Beans

Tony sat down at the dinner table with his family. He looked at his plate. He saw the roast beef and mashed potatoes, and he saw the corn on the cob, his favorite food. After the blessing, Tony started to eat.

"Tony," said Mother, "don't forget to eat your green beans."

Tony frowned. He had cleaned his plate, except for the green beans. "Do I really have to eat them?" he asked sheepishly. They looked like little green twigs on his plate.

"Try them," said Mother. "You should be thankful for all the food God has provided for us."

Tony ate one green bean and smiled. "It's good! I will eat them all!"

Thank you for the world so sweet,
Thank you for the food we eat.
Thank you for the birds that sing,
Thank you, God, for everything.

For every cup and plateful,
God, make us truly grateful!

Each time we eat,
may we remember
God's love.
Amen.

O Lord God, heavenly Father,
Bless us and these gifts,
which we shall accept from
Thy tender goodness.
Feed our souls with Your wisdom
so that we may partake
in Your heavenly table as well,
Lord Jesus Christ.

> Amen.

Bless, O Lord, Your gifts to our use
and us to Your service, for Christ's sake.

> Amen.

Thank You, Jesus

Dad usually said the blessing at breakfast, but today he asked everyone to share something they were thankful for. They all bowed their heads.

"Thank you, Jesus, for our food," said Teresa.

"Thank you for Mommy and Daddy," said Terry.

"Thank you, Jesus, for my friends," said Tony.

Mom and Dad prayed, too. Then it was Maria's turn to pray. Maria was the youngest. What could she thank Jesus for? she thought. "Jesus, thank you for... for... for EVERYONE!"

The family burst into laughter.

"Amen," they all said together. "Now, let's eat!"

We Plough the Fields, and Scatter

We plough the fields, and scatter
  The good seed on the land,
But it is fed and watered
  By God's almighty hand:
He sends the snow in winter,
  The warmth to swell the grain,
The breezes and the sunshine,
  And soft refreshing rain.

All good gifts around us
  Are sent from heaven above;
Then thank the Lord,
  O thank the Lord,
For all His love.

Give thanks to the Lord…who gives food
to every creature.

Psalm 136:1, 25

Be present at our table, Lord.
    Be here and everywhere adored.
His mercies bless and grant that we
    May strengthened for Thy service be.
Amen.

The Dinner Guest

Jonathan invited his friend to stay for dinner. Kevin was delighted. Jonathan's mom was a good cook. She always had good things to eat.

"Jonathan and Kevin," called Mother, "I need your help, please."

The boys hurried into the kitchen. Mother handed them a bag of corn. "Will you take these outside and shuck them for me?"

"You mean we have to do all that work?" said Kevin.

"We always help Mom," grinned Jonathan. "Here, you take this half and I'll finish them."

After supper, Kevin felt full and happy. He was proud that he had been a helper. It was fun to help prepare the family meal.

Come, Ye Thankful People

Come, ye thankful people, come—
   Raise the song of harvest home.
All is safely gathered in
   Ere the winter storms begin.
God, our Maker, doth provide
   For our wants to be supplied.
Come to God's own temple, come—
   Raise the song of harvest home.

All the world is God's own field,
   Fruit unto His praise to yield.
Wheat and tares together sown,
   Unto joy or sorrow grown.
First the blade and then the ear,
   Then the full corn shall appear.
Lord of harvest, grant that we
   Wholesome grain and pure may be.

Cake and candy are some of
God's most special treats.

God bless us, every one!

Charles Dickens

While they were eating,
Jesus took bread, gave thanks, and broke it.

Matthew 26:26

Thank you, O Lord,
for Thy gifts which
we are about to receive
from Thy bounty.

               Amen.

Teach Me, Jesus

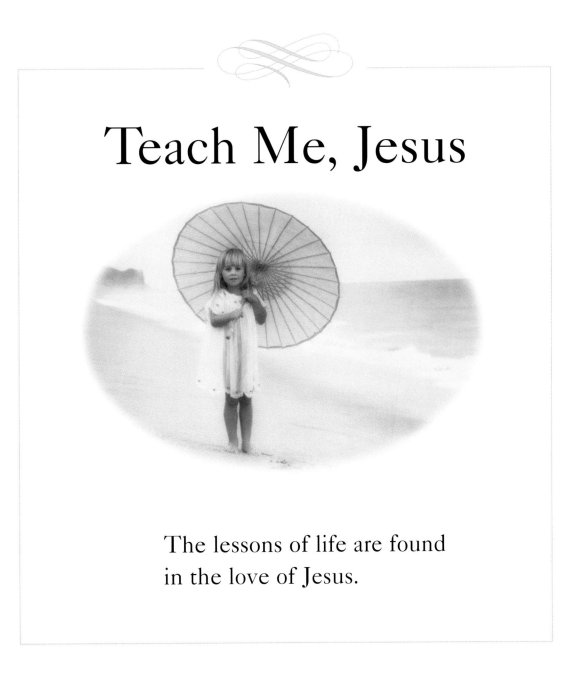

The lessons of life are found
in the love of Jesus.

A Baby Sister

"Benjamin, come meet your new baby sister," said Mother. All Benjamin could see was a blanket that wiggled. And it was Benjamin's blanket!

"Mommy, do I have to share *all* my things with the baby?" Benjamin pouted.

"You're a big brother now. Sharing and caring for your little sister is very important. See how small and helpless she is?" Benjamin peeked into the blanket and saw a tiny face and two little hands.

"Benjamin, can you hand me the baby's bottle? I think she's hungry."

Benjamin handed his mother the tiny bottle and curiously watched as the baby grabbed it with her dainty mouth.

"Thank you, Benjamin. You're such a good helper."

"Hmm, maybe a little sister's not so bad after all."

It's Me, O Lord

It's me, it's me, it's me, O Lord,
    Standing in the need of prayer.
It's me, it's me, O Lord,
    Standing in the need of prayer.

Not my brother or my sister,
    But it's me, O Lord,
Standing in the need of prayer.
    Not my brother or my sister,
But it's me, O Lord,
    Standing in the need of prayer.

'Tis the gift to be simple,
   'Tis the gift to be free,
'Tis the gift to come down
   Where we ought to be.
And when we find ourselves
   In the place just right,
'Twill be in the valley
   Of love and delight.
When true simplicity is gained
   To bow and to bend
We shall not be ashamed.
   To turn, turn will be our delight
Till by turning, turning,
   We come out right.

God is love, and we are His children.
There is no room for fear in love.
We love because He loved us first.

Dear Lord,
We pray not because we know how to pray,
but because we know our need of You.
Look kindly, Lord, on what we ask
and answer us when the time is right.

Amen.

God is not far from every one of us:
In Him we live and move and have our being.

To do to others as I would
 That they should do to me
Will make me gentle, kind, and good,
 As children ought to be.

Lord, You know that I love You.

St. John 21:16

Jesus said:

Blessed are the poor in spirit, for theirs
is the kingdom of heaven.

Blessed are they that mourn, for they
shall be comforted.

Blessed are the meek, for they shall
inherit the earth.

Blessed are they which do hunger and thirst
after righteousness, for they shall be filled.

Blessed are the merciful, for they shall obtain mercy.

Blessed are the pure in heart, for they shall see God.

Blessed are the peace-makers, for they shall be called
the children of God.

St. Matthew 5:1

Dear Lord,
Teach this child to pray,
and then accept my prayer.
You hear all the words I say
for You are everywhere.

                         Amen.

When I pray I speak to God,
when I listen God speaks to me.
I am now in His presence.
He is very near to me.

He Leadeth Me

He leadeth me!
   O blessed thought!
O words with heavenly
   comfort fraught!
Whatever I do,
Wherever I be,
   Still 'tis God's hand
   that leadeth me.

He leadeth me,
   He leadeth me,
By His own hand
   He leadeth me;
His faithful follower
I would be,
For by His hand
   He leadeth me.

Take Time to Be Holy

Take time to be holy,
  Speak often with thy Lord;
Abide in Him always
  And feed on His word.
Make friends of God's children,
  Help those who are weak,
Forgetting in nothing
  His blessing to seek.

Take time to be holy,
  The world rushes on;
Spend much time in secret
  With Jesus alone.
By looking to Jesus,
  Like Him thou shalt be;
Thy friends in thy conduct
  His likeness shall see.

Fair Share

Bryan grabbed the teddy bear away from his little sister. "My bear," said Nina with tears in her eyes. It was her bear, but Bryan was bored with his toys. He wanted something different.

Dad walked into the room. "My bear," Nina sobbed. "Bryan has my bear."

"Bryan," said Dad. "God wants you to share with your baby sister. If you are going to play with Nina's toy, why don't you offer her one of your toys?"

"Here Nina," said Bryan. "Would you like to play with my truck?"

"The truck?" Nina smiled reaching for the truck.

"Look Nina," Bryan grinned. "The bear can ride on the truck."

Under His Wings

Under His wings I am safely abiding.
  Though the night deepens
    and tempests are wild,
Still I can trust Him;
  I know He will keep me.
He has redeemed me, and I am His child.

Under His wings, under His wings,
  Who from His love can sever?
Under His wings my soul shall abide,
  Safely abide forever.

(continued)

Under His wings, what a refuge in sorrow!
How the heart yearningly turns to His rest!
Often when earth has no balm for my healing,
There I find comfort, and there I am blessed.

Under His wings, under His wings,
Who from His love can sever?
Under His wings my soul shall abide,
Safely abide forever.

Jesus Loves Me

Jesus loves me, this I know,
    For the Bible tells me so.
Little ones to Him belong.
    They are weak but He is strong.
Yes, Jesus loves me.
    Yes, Jesus loves me.
Yes, Jesus loves me,
    The Bible tells me so.

Tell Me the Story of Jesus

Tell me the story of Jesus,
   Write on my heart every word;
Tell me the story most precious,
   Sweetest that ever was heard.
Tell how the angels, in chorus,
   Sang as they welcomed His birth,
"Glory to God in the highest!
   Peace and good tidings to earth."

The Vow

Chris and Rachel sat on Rachel's porch with their Sunday school class. "Jesus just touched people and made them well. That's pretty neat," Chris said to Rachel.

"Yes, and remember that He was always kind to everyone. He loved His friends, but He loved His enemies, too," said Rachel.

"Do you think His friends were like you and me?" asked Chris.

"I'm sure of it. I hope that I can be as good a friend as Jesus was," said Rachel.

"You're always kind and you always share. Only Jesus can do miracles, but you can promise to always be kind," said Chris.

"Jesus would like that. You are such a good friend. You are like Jesus, too," said Rachel.

Footsteps of Jesus

Sweetly, Lord, have we heard Thee calling,
    "Come, follow Me!"
And we see where Thy footprints falling
    Lead us to Thee.
Footprints of Jesus, that make the pathway glow!
    We will follow the steps of Jesus wherever they go.

Though they lead over the cold, dark mountains,
    Seeking His sheep,
Or along by Siloam's fountains,
    Helping the weak:
Footprints of Jesus, that make the pathway glow!
    We will follow the steps of Jesus wherever they go.

They brought young children to Christ,
that He should touch them; and His disciples
rebuked those that brought them. But when Jesus saw it,
He was much displeased, and said unto them,
"Suffer the little children to come unto me,
and forbid them not; for of such is the kingdom of God.
Verily I say unto you, whosoever shall not receive
the kingdom of God as a little child, he shall not
enter therein." And He took them up in His arms,
put His hands upon them, and blessed them.

St. Mark 10:13

Dear Lord,
Please give me what I ask,
if You'd be glad about it.
But if You think it's not for me,
please help me do without it.

Help us to listen to Your voice.
Help us to be willing and quick
to do Your work.
Help us to be friendly and loving.
And help us to thank You every day
for all Your gifts to us.
Through Jesus Christ our Lord.

                   Amen.

Wonderful Words of Life

Sing them over again to me—
   Wonderful words of life;
Let me more of their beauty see—
   Wonderful words of life.
Words of life and beauty,
   Teach me faith and duty:
Beautiful words, wonderful words,
   Wonderful words of life.

Christ, the blessed One, gives to all
   Wonderful words of life;
Sinner, listen to the loving call—
   Wonderful words of life.
All so freely given,
   Wooing us to heaven:
Beautiful words, wonderful words,
   Wonderful words of life.

Our Father, who art in heaven,
hallowed be Thy name.
Thy kingdom come,
Thy will be done, on earth
as it is in heaven.
Give us this day our daily bread;
and forgive us our trespasses,
as we forgive those who trespass against us;
and lead us not into temptation,
but deliver us from evil.
For Thine is the kingdom,
and the power, and the glory,
for ever and ever. Amen.

Jesus Loves the Little Children

Jesus loves the little children,
　All the children of the world.
Red and yellow, black and white,
　They are precious in His sight.
Jesus loves the little children of the world.

Be Thou My Guardian

Be Thou my guardian and my guide,
　And hear me when I call;
Let not my slippery footsteps slide,
　And hold me lest I fall.

Jesus Loves All the Children

Cindy came home from school. She hugged her mother and kissed her on the cheek. "Mom, I have a new friend at school. His name is Frankie."

"I'm glad Frankie is your friend, Cindy."

"But Mom, the other children make fun of him. They say he doesn't wear nice clothes." Cindy was puzzled. "They tease him and make him cry. Mom, why don't they like him?"

"It sounds as though those children make fun of Frankie because his clothes are different than theirs," says Mom. "But you know that just because he wears different clothes doesn't mean he is bad or deserves to be teased. Jesus teaches us to love everyone the same way."

"Oh, I do, Mom. I love everyone, especially Frankie. I don't think Jesus likes it when the kids tease Frankie for being different. And I don't like it either."

God be in my head,

and in my understanding.

God be in my eyes,

and in my looking.

God be in my mouth,

and in my speaking.

God be in my heart,

and in my thinking.

God be at my end,

and at my departing.

Father, Lead Me Day by Day

Father, lead me day by day,
    Ever in Thine own sweet way;
Teach me to be pure and true;
    Show me what I ought to do.

When in danger, make me brave,
    Make me know that Thou can save;
Keep me safe by Thy dear side;
    Let me in Thy love abide.

When I'm tempted to do wrong,
    Make me steadfast, wise, and strong;
And when all alone I stand,
    Shield me with Thy mighty hand.
Amen.

Jesus Will Never Leave You

Tears filled Janet's large brown eyes. Things would never be the same again. Her best friend moved away. How sad she felt! "I miss her so much," cried Janet.

Mother saw how unhappy Janet was. She knew it was tough to have a friend move away. Mother put her arms around Janet's small shoulders. "I know how lonely you must feel, Janet," Mother whispered. "Some of my friends have moved away, too. But there is one friend who will never leave us. That friend is Jesus. So you see, darling, you are never really alone."

"Yes, Mom," Janet smiled up at Mother. "Jesus will always be with me."

More Love to Thee

More love to Thee, O Christ,
    More love to Thee!
Hear Thou the prayer I make
    On bended knee;
This is my earnest plea:

More love, O Christ, to Thee,
    More love to Thee,
More love to Thee!

Once earthly joy I craved,
    Sought peace and rest;
Now Thee alone I seek,
    Give what is best;
This all my prayer shall be;

More love, O Christ, to Thee,
    More love to Thee,
More love to Thee!

Dear God,
Be good to me.
The sea is so wide,
and my boat is so small.

All for You, dear God,
everything I do, or think,
or say, the whole day long.
Help me to be good.

I Must Tell Jesus

I must tell Jesus all of my trials,
    I cannot bear these burdens alone;
In my distress He kindly will help me,
    He ever loves and cares for His own.

I must tell Jesus!
    I must tell Jesus!
I cannot bear my burdens alone;
    I must tell Jesus!
I must tell Jesus!
    Jesus can help me, Jesus alone.

Father, Hear the Prayer We Offer

Father, hear the prayer we offer:
    Not for ease that prayer shall be,
But for strength that we may ever
    Live our lives courageously.

Not for ever in green pastures
    Do we ask our way to be;
But the steep and rugged pathway
    May we tread rejoicingly.

Not for ever by still waters
    Would we idly rest and stay;
But would smite the living fountains
    From the rocks along our way.

Be our strength in hours of weakness,
    In our wanderings be our guide;
Through endeavor, failure, danger,
    Father, be Thou at our side.

By the prayers of Jesus, Lord teach us how to pray.

By the gifts of Jesus, Lord teach us how to give.

By the toils of Jesus, Lord teach us how to work.

By the love of Jesus, Lord teach us how to love.

By the cross of Jesus, Lord teach us how to live.

Good Lord,

Help me to win if I may,

and if I may not,

help me to be a good loser.

Jesus Is All the World to Me

Jesus is all the world to me,
　　My life, my joy, my all;
He is my strength from day to day,
　　Without Him I would fall:
When I am sad, to Him I go,
　　No other one can cheer me so;
When I am sad He makes me glad,
　　He's my friend.

Jesus is all the world to me,
　　My friend in trials sore;
I go to Him for blessings,
　　And He gives them over and over:
He sends the sunshine and the rain,
　　He sends the harvest's golden grain;
Sunshine and rain, harvest of grain,
　　He's my friend.
Amen.

Lead Us, Heavenly Father, Lead Us

Lead us, heavenly Father, lead us
    Over the world's tempestuous sea;
Guard us, guide us, keep us, feed us,
    For we have no help but Thee;
Yet possessing every blessing
    If our God our Father be.

Lord of the loving heart,
may mine be loving, too.
Lord of the gentle hands,
may mine be gentle, too.
Lord of the willing feet,
may mine be willing, too.
So may I grow more like Thee
in all I say and do.

Dear Lord, teach this child to pray,
and then accept my prayer.
You hear all the words I say
for You are everywhere.

Jesus and Me

O praise Jesus, for He
is with us everywhere.

Sunshine in My Soul

There is sunshine in my soul today,
    More glorious and bright
Than glows in any earthly sky,
    For Jesus is my light.

O there's sunshine, blessed sunshine,
    When the peaceful, happy moments roll;
When Jesus shows His smiling face,
    There is sunshine in my soul.

There is music in my soul today,
    A carol to my King,
And Jesus, listening, can hear
    The songs I cannot sing.

O there's sunshine, blessed sunshine,
    When the peaceful, happy moments roll;
When Jesus shows His smiling face,
    There is sunshine in my soul.

What can I give Him,
  Poor as I am?
If I were a shepherd,
  I would bring a lamb;
If I were a wise man,
  I would do my part;
Yet what I can I give Him—
  Give my heart.

Christina Rossetti

Others there are who go to sea in ships
and make their living on the wide waters.
These men have seen the acts of the Lord
and His marvelous doings in the deep.
At His command the storm wind rose
and lifted the waves high.
So they cried to the Lord in their trouble,
and He brought them out of their distress.
The storm sank to a murmur
and the waves of the sea were stilled.
Let them thank the Lord for His enduring love
and for the marvelous things He has done for men.

Psalm 107

Be Not Dismayed Whatever Betide

Be not dismayed whatever betide,
    God will take care of you;
Beneath His wings of love abide,
    God will take care of you.

God will take care of you,
    Through every day,
Over all the way;
    He will take care of you,
God will take care of you.
    Amen.

Peace Like a River

I've got peace like a river,
   I've got peace like a river,
I've got peace like a river in my soul.
   I've got peace like a river,
I've got peace like a river,
   I've got peace like a river in my soul.

I've got love like an ocean,
   I've got love like an ocean,
I've got love like an ocean in my soul.
   I've got love like an ocean,
I've got love like an ocean,
   I've got love like an ocean in my soul.

I've got joy like a fountain,
   I've got joy like a fountain,
I've got joy like a fountain in my soul.
   I've got joy like a fountain,
I've got joy like a fountain,
   I've got joy like a fountain in my soul.

Love Divine, All Loves Excelling

Love divine, all loves excelling,
    Joy of heaven, to earth come down,
Fix in us Thy humble dwelling,
    All Thy faithful mercies crown.
Jesus, Thou art all compassion,
    Pure unbounded love Thou art;
Visit us with Thy salvation,
    Enter every trembling heart.

God Moves in a Mysterious Way

God moves in a mysterious way
    His wonders to perform;
He plants his footsteps in the sea,
    And rides upon the storm.

Deep in unfathomable mines
    Of never-failing skill,
He treasures up his bright designs,
    And works his sovereign will.

Ye fearful saints, fresh courage take,
    The clouds ye so much dread
Are big with mercy, and shall break
    In blessings on your head.

O Worship the King

O worship the King
　All glorious above;
O gratefully sing
　His power and His love.
Our shield and defender,
　The ancient of days,
Pavilioned in splendor,
　And girded with praise.

O tell of His might,
　O sing of His grace,
Whose robe is the light,
　Whose canopy space.
His chariots of wrath
　The deep thunderclouds form,
And dark is His path
　On the wings of the storm.

Jesus, Priceless Treasure

Jesus, priceless treasure,
    Source of purest pleasure,
Truest friend to me;
    Long my heart hath panted,
Till it well-nigh fainted,
    Thirsting after Thee.
Thine I am, O spotless Lamb,
    I will suffer naught to hide Thee,
Ask for naught beside Thee.

Wonderful, Wonderful Jesus

There is never a day so dreary,
    There is never a night so long,
But the soul that is trusting Jesus
    Will somewhere find a song.

Wonderful, wonderful Jesus,
    In the heart He implanteth a song:
A song of deliverance, of courage, of strength,
    In the heart He implanteth a song.

What a Friend We Have in Jesus

What a friend we have in Jesus,
   All our sins and griefs to bear,

What a privilege to carry
   Everything to God in prayer.

O what peace we often forfeit,
   O what needless pain we bear,

All because we do not carry
   Everything to God in prayer.

Praise Him, All Ye Little Children

Praise Him, praise Him, all ye little children;
  God is Love, God is Love.
Praise Him, praise Him, all ye little children;
  God is Love, God is Love.

Love Him, love Him, all ye little children;
  God is Love, God is Love.
Love Him, love Him, all ye little children;
  God is Love, God is Love.

Serve Him, serve Him, all ye little children;
  God is Love, God is Love.
Serve Him, serve Him, all ye little children;
  God is Love, God is Love.

The Name of Jesus

The name of Jesus is so sweet,
  I love its music to repeat.
It makes my joys full and complete,
  The precious name of Jesus.

"Jesus," O how sweet the name!
  "Jesus," every day the same.
"Jesus," let all saints proclaim
  Its worthy praise forever.

I love the name of Him whose heart
  Knows all my griefs, and bears a part.
Who bids all anxious fears depart
  I love the name of Jesus.

"Jesus," O how sweet the name!
  "Jesus," every day the same.
"Jesus," let all saints proclaim
  Its worthy praise forever.

O praise God in His holiness: praise Him in the firmament of His power.

Praise Him in His noble acts: praise Him according to His excellent greatness.

Praise Him in the sound of the trumpet: praise Him upon the lute and harp.

Praise Him in the cymbals and dances: praise Him upon the strings and pipe.

Praise Him upon the well-tuned cymbals: praise Him upon the loud cymbals.

Let every thing that hath breath: praise the Lord.

Psalm 150

Praise to the Lord, the Almighty

Praise to the Lord, the Almighty,
    The King of creation;
O my soul, praise Him,
    For He is thy health and salvation.
Come, ye who hear,
    Brothers and sisters, draw near,
Praise Him in glad adoration.

O for a Closer Walk with God

O for a closer walk with God,
    A calm and heavenly frame;
A light to shine upon the road
    That leads me to the Lamb!

There Is a Land of Pure Delight

There is a land of pure delight
   Where saints immortal reign;
Infinite day excludes the night,
   And pleasures banish pain.

There everlasting spring abides,
   And never-withering flowers;
Death, like a narrow sea, divides
   This heavenly land from ours.

A Shelter in the Time of Storm

The Lord's our Rock, in Him we hide—
    A shelter in the time of storm;
Secure whatever ill betide—
    A shelter in the time of storm.

O Jesus is a Rock in a weary land,
    A weary land, a weary land;
O Jesus is a Rock in a weary land—
    A shelter in the time of storm.

A shade by day, defense by night—
    A shelter in the time of storm;
No fears alarm, no foes affright—
    A shelter in the time of storm.

O Jesus is a Rock in a weary land,
    A weary land, a weary land;
O Jesus is a Rock in a weary land—
    A shelter in the time of storm.

When I pray to You, Jesus Christ,
my fingers fold together as if
to say "Hello" to one another,
just as I am saying "Hello" to You.

The grace of our Lord Jesus Christ,
and the love of God, and the fellowship
of the Holy Ghost be with us all evermore.

2 Corinthians 13:14

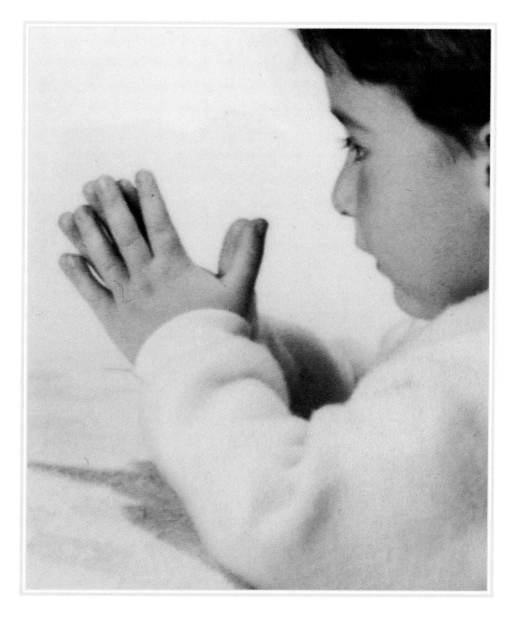

God is Light:
and in Him is no darkness at all.

God is not far from every one of us:
in Him we live and move and have our being.

The peace of God, which passeth
all understanding, keep your hearts
and minds in the knowledge and
love of God, and of His Son, Jesus Christ
our Lord: And the blessing of God Almighty,
the Father, the Son, and the Holy Ghost,
be amongst you and remain with you always.

Praise Jesus for every child.
Each one's different and each one's special.
You help to keep the precious children safe
and love them with all Your heart.
May each child know that love of Yours
and share that love with each other.
May each child look at one another
and not see "different," but "brother."

I want to make this basket, Jesus.
Please help to give me focus.
Every time I throw the ball,
it lands behind me.
I know You are pretty busy, Lord,
but will You please help?
If I don't make it in the basket
today, I'll understand.
Maybe I'll try again tomorrow.

Dear Jesus,
Sunflowers are the sweetest flowers
I have seen. Did You name them
sunflowers because they are the color
of the sun, or because they are as big
as the sun? When I look up in the morning,
I like to picture my flowers rising up
over the trees. Thank you for the morning
and for sunflowers.

Amen.

There is no Holy One like the Lord;

there is no one besides You;

there is no Rock like our God.

1 Samuel 2:2

God's Wonderful World

The love of God is shown
in the beauty of the earth.

The World Needs a Drink

Jacob loved to play outside. He played with his trucks in the sandbox. He climbed on his fort. He liked to swing on his swing set. Everything was fun for him. Jacob just wanted to be outside in the fresh air.

"Jacob," Mother called, "it's starting to rain. You will have to come inside."

"I don't want to come in," said Jacob frowning. "Let me stay outside!"

"I'm sorry, Jacob," Mother explained. "But you must come inside until the rain stops. God made the rain so the world could have a drink. Why don't you come in for a drink of water, too?"

What do the stars do
    Up in the sky,
Higher than the wind can blow,
    Or the clouds can fly?

Each star in its own glory
    Circles, circles still;
As it was lit to shine and set,
    And do its Maker's will.

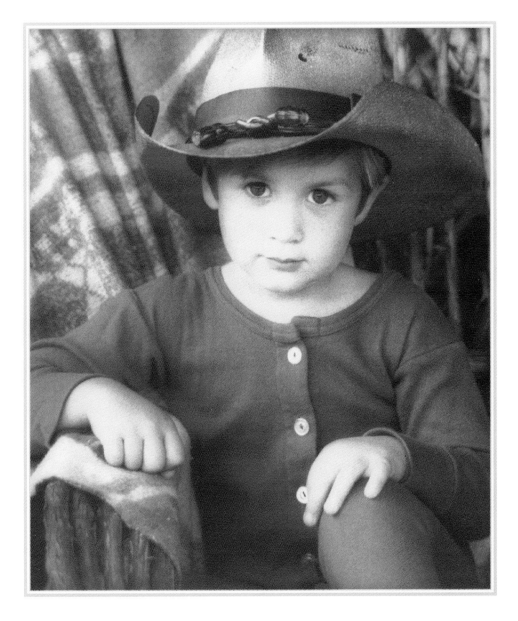

For rosy apples, juicy plums,
    And yellow pears so sweet,
For hips and haws on bush and hedge,
    And flowers at our feet,
For ears of corn all ripe and dry,
    And colored leaves on trees,
We thank You, heavenly Jesus Christ,
    For such good gifts as these.

The Colors in the Sky

Two children sat on a park bench watching the sun slowly slip down into the trees. "The sun is going to bed so the moon can come out to play," explained Terri.

The sky was blazing with bright orange, red, and pink. John looked at his friend. "The sky looks like fire!" said John pointing to the sunset. "Will it burn the moon?"

"It's not on fire, John," said Terri. "God gives us beautiful colors at the end of the day to remember at night when the sky is dark."

"That's neat," said John. "Thank you, Jesus, for the beautiful colors in the sky."

I Never Saw a Moor

I never saw a moor,
 I never saw the sea;
Yet know I how the heather looks,
 And what a wave must be.

I never spoke with God,
 Nor visited in heaven;
Yet certain am I of the spot
 As if the chart were given.

Emily Dickinson

Dear Jesus,
Who has made all things beautiful:
give me a love of Thy countryside, its lanes
and meadows, its woods and streams, and
clean open spaces; and let me keep it fresh and
unspoiled for those who shall come after me.

Amen.

Keep us, O Lord, as the apple of Your eye;
hide us under the shadow of Your wings.

When the weather is wet,
   We must not fret.
When the weather is cold,
   We must not scold.
When the weather is warm,
   We must not storm.
Be thankful together,
   Whatever the weather.

In the Garden

I come to the garden alone,
    While the dew is still on the roses.
And the voice I hear,
    Falling on my ear,
The Son of God discloses.

And He walks with me,
    And He talks with me,
And He tells me I am His own.
    And the joy we share
As we tarry there,
    None other has ever known.

Making Music

Maria walked through the field humming to herself. As she walked, the sound of her legs rustled softly against the tall grass. She watched flocks of birds land for a moment, then flutter back into the air. Other birds sat in a tree and sang little songs. The soft breeze seemed to whistle a soft tune in her ears. Maria could hear crickets chirping their special little song in the grass. In the distance, a woodpecker tapped out a steady rhythm.

Maria felt happy as she listened to God's melodies around her. She thought to herself, "Jesus has a way of making music that is just perfect for a walk on a beautiful summer day!"

God bless the field and bless the lane,
    Stream and branch and lion's mane,
Hill and stone and flower and tree,
    From every end of my country—
Bless the sun and bless the sleet,
    Bless the road and bless the street,
Bless the night and bless the day,
    In each and every tiny way;
Bless the minnow, bless the whale,
    Bless the rainbow and the hail,
Bless the nest and bless the leaf,
    Bless the righteous and the thief,
Bless the wing and bless the fin,
    Bless the air I travel in,
Bless the mill and bless the mouse,
    Bless the miller's bricken house,
Bless the earth and bless the sea,
    God bless you and God bless me.

Jesus Shall Reign Wherever the Sun

Jesus shall reign wherever the sun
    Does His successive journeys run;
His kingdom stretch from shore to shore
    Till moons shall wax and wane no more.
Let every creature rise and bring
    Peculiar honors to our King;
Angels descend with songs again,
    And earth repeat the long amen.

A Hill of Flowers

"Let's go play on the hill," said Tammy, motioning to her best friend.

"Wait, Tammy, wait!" called Rebecca.

Tammy stopped and waited for Rebecca to catch up with her. At last they both stood at the top of the hill. The hill was covered with colorful flowers. How sweet they smelled!

"God made the flowers, didn't He?" asked Rebecca, leaning over to smell a daisy.

"Jesus must love us very much to give us such a wonderful place to play," Tammy said.

Both children plopped to the ground. The soft grass tickled their bare toes. "Come on, Rebecca," said Tammy, "let's roll down the hill! Weeeeeeee!"

For the Beauty of the Earth

For the beauty of the earth,
    For the glory of the skies,
For the love which from our birth
    Over and around us lies:
Christ our God, to Thee we raise
    This our hymn of grateful praise.

For the wonder of each hour
    Of the day and of the night,
Hill and vale and tree and flower,
    Sun and moon and stars of light:
Christ our God, to Thee we raise
    This our hymn of grateful praise.

Thank God for rain
and the beautiful rainbow colors.
And thank God for letting children
splash in puddles.

The Lord is good to me,
and so I thank the Lord
for giving me the things I need:
the sun, the rain, and the apple seed!
The Lord is good to me.

The New Kite

Mark ran as fast as he could. The kite bounced on the ground. Was it flying? No, just bouncing.

Mark could not understand. Dad had made his kite. It was the best kite in the whole world. It had a long tail. He had a big ball of string. He could run fast. So why wouldn't his kite fly?

Suddenly the kite bounced again and lifted up into the air. Mark held his string and watched the kite soar even higher. Mark knew that God made the wind. "Thank you, Jesus, for sending the wind to fly my kite!"

Let All the World in Every Corner Sing

Let all the world in every corner sing,
    My God and King!
The heavens are not too high,
    His praise may thither fly;
The earth is not too low,
    His praises there may grow.
Let all the world in every corner sing,
    My God and King!

Pied Beauty

Glory be to God for dappled things—
　　For skies of couple-color as a brindled cow;
For rose-moles all in stipple upon trout that swim;
　　Fresh-firecoal chestnut-falls; finches' wings;
Landscape plotted and pieced—fold, fallow, and plough;
　　And all trades, their gear and tackle and trim.

All things counter, original, spare, strange;
　　Whatever is fickle, freckled (who knows how?)
With swift, slow; sweet, sour; adazzle, dim;
　　He fathers-forth whose beauty is past change:
Praise Him.

Gerard Manley Hopkins

Fall Is Here

The colorful leaves floated silently to the ground like snowflakes. "But snowflakes are all white," thought Audrey. "I love to watch the leaves flutter down in the wind. There's an orange leaf. And a red one. Maybe I can catch it." Audrey reached for the red leaf and laughed as the wind lifted it back up into the air.

The leaves were all around Audrey. She plopped down into a soft pile her friend, Tommy, had raked up earlier. "Thank you, Jesus," she thought happily as she gazed at the wonder of color. "Thank you for painting the leaves. It's such a beautiful way of telling us that fall is here."

God made the sun,
  And God made the trees.
God made the mountains,
  And God made me.

Thank you, O God,
  For the sun and the trees,
For making the mountains,
  And for making me.

All People That on Earth Do Dwell

All people that on earth do dwell,
    Sing to the Lord with cheerful voice;
Him serve with mirth, His praise forth tell,
    Come ye before Him, and rejoice.

The Lord, ye know, is God indeed;
    Without our aid He did us make;
We are His folk, He doth us feed,
    And for His sheep He doth us take.

Jesus, if I were a flower
   Instead of a little child,
I would choose my home by a waterfall,
   To laugh at its gambols wild,
(To be sprinkled with spray and dew;)
   And I'd be a harebell blue.

Blue is the color of heaven,
   And blue is the color for me.
But in the rough earth my clinging roots
   Closely nestled should be;
For the earth is friendly and true
   To the little harebell blue.

Father, We Thank Thee

For flowers that bloom about our feet,
    Father, we thank Thee,
For tender grass so fresh and sweet,
    Father, we thank Thee,
For the song of bird and hum of bee,
    For all things fair we hear or see,
Father in heaven, we thank Thee.

(continued)

For blue of stream and blue of sky,
   Father, we thank Thee,
For pleasant shade of branches high,
   Father, we thank Thee,
For fragrant air and cooling breeze,
   For beauty of the blooming trees,
Father in heaven, we thank Thee.

For this new morning with its light,
   Father, we thank Thee,
For rest and shelter of the night,
   Father, we thank Thee,
For health and food, for love and friends,
   For everything Thy goodness sends,
Father in heaven, we thank Thee.

Ralph Waldo Emerson

The trees are shedding all their leaves,
    Soon it will grow colder.
O dear Jesus, be with me—
    Your love wrapped round my shoulder.

As You keep me snuggled tight,
    I'll sit and watch the trees.
For they might get chilled at night,
    Without their blankets green.

When to the flowers so beautiful the Father gave a name,
  Back came a little blue-eyed one, all timidly she came.
And standing at the Father's feet and gazing in His face
  She said in low and trembling tones,
"Dear God, the name Thou gave to me, alas, I have forgot."
  Then kindly looked the Father down and said,
  "Forget Me not."

All God's Creatures

Fuzzy, feathered, or finned,
Jesus loves every creature.

Did Jesus Have a Puppy Too?

"Oh, Laddie, you are so beautiful! You're the cutest puppy in the whole world!" Lauren sat on the floor petting and hugging the furry little puppy. "I love you!"

Laddie was a birthday present for Lauren. "It's my best birthday ever!" thought Lauren. Laddie snuggled against her. His big brown eyes sparkled as his tiny tongue licked her face like a soft kiss.

"Mommy," Lauren called to her mother who was sitting in a chair next to her. "I'm so happy that God made little puppies. Do you think that Jesus had a puppy when He was a little boy?"

Something so tiny as a butterfly
can hold all the love of Jesus.

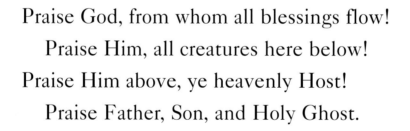

Praise God, from whom all blessings flow!
Praise Him, all creatures here below!
Praise Him above, ye heavenly Host!
Praise Father, Son, and Holy Ghost.

If a rabbit had words,
it would thank You for its ears.
If an elephant had words,
it would thank You for its trunk.
If a zebra had words,
it would thank You for its stripes.
If a cat had words,
it would thank You for its whiskers.
But since only I have words, dear Jesus,
I will thank You for them all!

A Visit to the Zoo

"I love the zoo!" Margaret chattered happily as she skipped from one place to another. She noticed how different the animals were. "Look at the big hippo. Look at the tall giraffe with the long, skinny neck!"

Grandmother smiled as Margaret observed the animals. "The zebra has stripes. The leopard has spots. I love the elephant's long nose."

Margaret paused and looked at her grandmother. "Did God make ALL the animals?"

"Yes, God made them all."

"Does God love the animals the same way even when they're different?"

"Yes," Grandmother smiled. "And He loves all the children in the world, even when they're different."

Hear my prayer, Lord Jesus,
for our friends the animals.
Give to them all Thy mercy and pity,
and all compassion from those who
deal with them.
Make all hands that touch them gentle,
and all voices that speak to them kind.
Help us to be true friends to animals,
so that we may share the blessings
of Thy mercy.
For the sake of tender-hearted Jesus Christ
our Lord.

Trees

I think that I shall never see
  A poem lovely as a tree.

A tree whose hungry mouth is pressed
  Against the earth's sweet flowing breast;

A tree that looks at God all day,
  And lifts her leafy arms to pray;

A tree that may in summer wear
  A nest of robins in her hair;

Upon whose bosom snow has lain;
  Who intimately lives with rain.

Poems are made by fools like me,
  But only God can make a tree.

Joyce Kilmer

You are to me, O Lord,
what wings are to the flying bird.

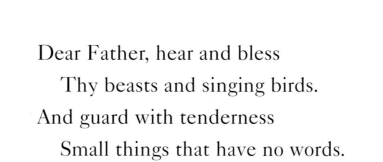

Dear Father, hear and bless
   Thy beasts and singing birds.
And guard with tenderness
   Small things that have no words.

A Home for Boomer

Malcom saw a dog. "Where did you come from?" Malcom stooped to pet the dog. "Are you lost? You can come live with me. I'll name you Boomer."

"Mommy, Mommy! Look what I found! May I keep Boomer, Mommy, please?!"

Mother reached down and scratched Boomer's ears. She noticed the collar and tag. "Malcom, I know you really want Boomer, but he already has a home. We'd better take him back to his own family."

"He has a family?"

"Yes, and they are probably worried about him. Jesus would want the dog to be with his own family."

"You found Jasper!" said the owners. "Oh, thank you! We've missed him so much."

"You know, Mom, I think Jesus is glad we took Boomer back to his home. Bringing Boomer home was the right thing to do."

The Lamb

Little lamb, who made thee?
    Dost thou know who made thee;
Gave thee life and bid thee feed
    By the stream and over the mead;
Gave thee clothing of delight,
    Softest clothing, woolly, bright;
Gave thee such a tender voice
    Making all the vales rejoice?
Little lamb, who made thee?
    Dost thou know who made thee?

(continued)

Little lamb, I'll tell thee,
    Little lamb, I'll tell thee:
He is called by thy name,
    For He calls Himself a Lamb.
He is meek and He is mild;
    He became a little child.
I a child and thou a lamb,
    We are called by His name.
Little lamb, God bless thee.
    Little lamb, God bless thee.

William Blake

The Hungry Kitten

"Martin, have you fed your kitten?" asked Mother.

"I forgot."

"Remember, you promised to take care of your kitten if we let you keep her."

"I'll do it tomorrow. I want to play now."

"Meow," said the hungry kitten.

Martin looked at the tiny kitten. She looked so helpless. She didn't have a mommy to take care of her. "God made this kitten and God made me," Martin said to himself. "Jesus would want me to care for her just like He cares for me!"

"Meow."

"I think Jesus wants me to feed my kitten right now. Mommy, where's the cat food?"

The Princess and the Frog

"And the princess kissed the frog and he turned into a handsome prince. They got married and lived happily ever after." Mother closed the book and leaned over to kiss Gretchen good night.

"Oh, Mom, no one could kiss a frog!" Gretchen's face twisted into a frown. "They are so gross!"

"But Gretchen," explained her mother, "God made frogs and many other creatures. Jesus loves them all. None of them are gross to Him."

"I never thought of it like that. But Mom, do I have to love them?"

"You should love all God's creatures, Gretchen, but you don't have to kiss them!"

Lord Jesus,
Bless my tiny puppy
as he sits at home all day.
For he is so brave and believes himself
to be a great watchdog, while still so small.

Dear Jesus,
Sometimes all I need to do is
look at my dog watching me,
and I know I am being taken care of,
in more ways than one.

All things bright and beautiful,
  All creatures great and small,
All things wise and wonderful,
  The Lord God made them all.

Cecil Frances Alexander

The birds above me;
the kitten on my lap;
the toad that hops;
the deer that runs;
Lord Jesus, it was You who
created all these wonderful animals.
Thank you, Lord.
They are treasured.

Squirrels are God's Creatures

"Come on, Sheba," called Mark. "Let's go for a walk." Sheba wagged her tail and bounded after Mark. The leaves rustled as they tromped through the yard. Fat squirrels with busy tails chattered and scampered around the yard, gathering food for the winter.

Suddenly Sheba bounded toward one of the squirrels, barking wildly. The frightened squirrel scurried up a tree as Sheba barked.

"Stop!" Mark called. Sheba stopped barking and looked up at Mark's disappointed face. "Oh, Sheba," scolded Mark. "You shouldn't frighten the squirrels. Don't you know that squirrels are God's creatures? I think we'd better go inside now and let the squirrels gather their food in peace."

He prayeth best, who loveth best
All things both great and small;
For the dear God who loveth us,
He made and loveth all.

Friends in Jesus

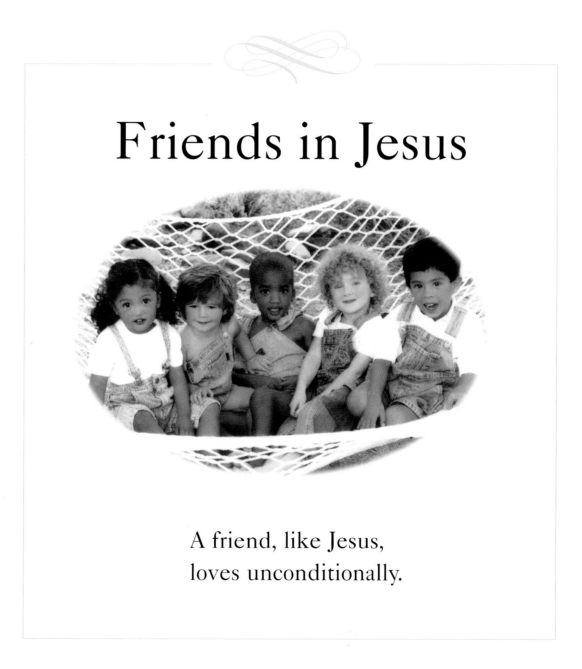

A friend, like Jesus,
loves unconditionally.

Food Tastes Better When It's Shared

Zac and Katy sat down to eat the snacks Mother had fixed for them. "Oh boy! I've got popcorn. It's my favorite," said Zac.

"I've got raisins. They're my favorite."

"Would you like some popcorn, Katy?" Zac held out a handful of popcorn.

"Oh, yes please! Would you like some raisins?" asked Katy. She gave a handful of raisins to Zac. Soon both Zac and Katy had a tasty mixture of popcorn and raisins.

"Look what we made," said Katy. "Mmm, it's good."

"Food tastes *better* when it's shared!"

A friend is someone who doesn't judge.

A friend is someone who loves me for me.

A friend can play and make me happy,

but a friend also understands when I can't play.

You are my friend, Jesus.

Thank You for being my friend.

Dear friends, since God so loved us,
we also ought to love one another.

I John 4:11

Lord Jesus Christ,
Teach me the ways of friendship
so that I may be a good friend
to someone who needs me,
just like You.

My friend is special to me,
Lord Jesus, please help me to
keep her in my heart until we grow old.

Are We Still Good Friends?

Christopher and Matthew were playing cards together at Christopher's house. It was fun until Matthew began taking cards from the deck and putting them in his pile.

"You can't do that!" said Christopher. "That's cheating!"

"But I want to win!"

"It is fun to win, but cheating to win is not right. Cheating is like stealing. The Bible says not to steal."

"I'm sorry. I never thought of it like that. Are we still good friends?"

"Yes. I forgive you. We can play some more if you promise not to cheat again."

"I promise. Let's start over."

Friends Are Helpers

Deena went to Stan's house to play. It was always fun to visit Stan. He had lots of great toys. Deena knocked on the door.

"Hello, Deena," said Stan's mother. "I'm afraid that Stan won't be able to play with you today. He has to clean up his room before he can play."

"Oh," said Deena sadly. She thought for a minute. "May I help him clean up his room? I always clean my room at home."

"I'm sure Stan could use some help, but remember, no playing until the room is clean. Stan," she called, "your friend Deena is here to help you clean your room."

Dear Lord,
Make me the sort of person
who causes other people to feel happier,
whatever I feel like myself.

Thank you for my friend next door,
   And my friend across the street,
And please help me to be a friend
   To everyone I meet.

I feel lonely today, Jesus.

Everyone else seems to have friends, but I don't.

Help me to know that You, Jesus Christ, are a

friend to everyone and that You are the

best friend I could ever hope for.

With You by my side, I know that I am

never truly alone.

A friend loves at all times.

Proverbs 17:17a

My Best Friend

"Mommy, who is your best friend?" Casey asked as she crawled up onto her mother's lap. Casey and her tattered teddy bear snuggled close to Mother.

"I guess your daddy is my best friend, next to Jesus."

"I have a best friend. I can always talk to Him. He helps me do the right thing. He is always with me when ever I need Him."

"That sounds like a good friend, Casey. Who is He?"

Mother looked at Casey's teddy bear and smiled.

"Jesus is my best friend!" Casey hugged her teddy bear. "And Teddy is my *next* best friend."

Friends come in all shapes and sizes.
My best friend is also my brother.
Thank you, Jesus, for giving me
such a great best friend who lives
so close that we can play all the time.
I couldn't have asked for a better
friend, except if that friend were You,
Jesus, because You are everyone's
friend; so kind and loving, too.
Do You want to play with us sometime?

May the road rise to meet you,

may the wind be always at your back,

may the sun shine warm on your face,

the rain fall softly on your fields;

and until we meet again,

may God hold you in the palm of His hand.

Lord Jesus,

Help me never to judge another

until I have walked many miles in his shoes.

Jesus, friend of the little children,
    Be a friend to me.
Take my hand and ever keep me
    Close to Thee.

Teach me how to grow in goodness
    Daily, as I grow.
Thou has been a child,
    And surely Thou dost know.

Never leave me nor forsake me,
    Ever be my friend,
For I need Thee from life's dawning
    To its end.

A Friend by Your Side

"I'm glad you're my friend," said Adam.

"I'm glad you're my friend, too," said Heather. "Let's go play in the park." The two children walked to the small park next to Adam's house.

Adam and Heather went to the same school. They had the same teacher. They did everything together! They were best friends. When Adam told a joke, Heather laughed the loudest. When Heather was sad, Adam would always cheer her up.

They sat on a stone wall and looked at the flowers in the park. Butterflies flitted about together.

"Look at those two butterflies," said Adam. "Do you think they are best friends, too?"

The Favorite Doll

Rachel and Melissa were playing at Rachel's house with their new dolls. Rachel's room was filled with dolls of all kinds. There were big dolls and little dolls, baby dolls and grown-up dolls. Melissa looked at all the dolls and hugged her doll, Betsy, close to her.

Rachel put her new doll down and asked to hold Betsy. Melissa didn't want to give Betsy up. "No," she said. "I want to keep Betsy."

"It would be fun to share!" said Rachel. "Here, you can play with Dolly. She's my favorite doll."

Dolly looked lonesome. "OK. We'll trade dolls for a little while."

"See, sharing is fun," grinned Rachel. "My favorite doll for your favorite doll."

A friend is someone you can trust,
even with a very important secret.
A friend will always be there,
even when times are tough.
A friend will play your favorite game,
even if it isn't her favorite.
A friend forgives you when you're wrong
and even loves you in the end.
A friend is someone truly special,
just like You, Lord Jesus Christ.

Dear Jesus,
Friends like us don't happen
by accident. I know that You
sent me my two best friends.
But how did You know that
my favorite game to play is cowboy?
I guess You just know these things.
Thank you, Jesus, for my friends.

                Amen.

Dear Jesus,
Thank you for my friend.
I know my friend is here to
comfort me when You can't be
here Yourself.

Bedtime Blessings

The love and comfort of Jesus
surrounds us as we sleep.

Puppy Dog Dreams

"Good night, Buttons," said Lisa as she tucked her stuffed dog into his cozy little bed. "Sweet dreams!" Lisa thought for a minute. "I wonder if stuffed animals have dreams."

When Lisa's mother came in to hear her prayers, Lisa asked her if stuffed animals dream.

"Lisa, I don't think they have dreams," explained her mother.

"That is sad. I have such good dreams. I think I will ask Jesus to let me have dreams for my stuffed dog since he can't have dreams of his own." Lisa began to pray, "Dear Jesus, I know my stuffed dog cannot dream on his own, so please let me dream about grassy parks and big, tall trees, and all his puppy friends for him. Thank you very much. Amen."

Matthew, Mark, Luke, and John
   Bless the bed that I lie on.
Before I lay me down to sleep,
   I give my soul to Christ to keep.
Four corners to my bed,
   Four angels overspread:
One at the head, one at the feet,
   And two to guard me while I sleep.
I go by sea, I go by land,
   The Lord made me with His right hand.
If any danger come to me,
   Sweet Jesus Christ, deliver me.
He is the branch and I'm the flower,
   May God send me a happy hour.

Be near me, Lord Jesus; I ask Thee to stay
    Close by me forever, and love me, I pray;
Bless all the dear children in Thy tender care,
    And fit us for heaven to live with Thee there.

Angels at the foot,
    And angels at the head,
And like a curly little lamb
    My pretty babe in bed.

A Monster in My Closet

"There's a monster in my room!" David peeked out from under the covers. His heart was pounding. "Grrrrr!" roared the monster.

The monster was in his closet! David pulled up the covers higher over his head. "Grrrrr!" roared the monster again. What should David do?

"Dear Jesus, Mommy says that You are always with me. Please help me not to be afraid." David slipped out from under the covers. He was trembling, but he knew that Jesus would protect him. He opened the closet door slowly.

"Grrrrrr," growled his little puppy shaking an old shoe in his mouth. "Grrrrr."

"Oh, Baxter," David laughed, "it's just you."

Glory to Thee, My God, This Night

Glory to Thee, my God, this night
  For all the blessing of the light;
Keep me, O keep me, King of Kings,
  Beneath Thy own almighty wings.

Forgive me, Lord, for Thy dear Son,
  The ill that I this day have done,
That with the world, myself, and Thee,
  I, before I sleep, at peace may be.

In my little bed I lie,
    God, my Father, hear my cry;
Please protect me through the night,
    Keep me safe till morning light.
Amen.

Bye, baby bunting,
    Thy father's gone a-hunting.
He's gone to catch a moonbeam bright
    To guard you as you sleep tonight.

A Doll Won't Run Away

Diane loved her new kitten. She put it in a doll carriage and rolled it around the playroom. At bedtime, Diane hugged the fluffy, purring kitten and they snuggled into the soft bed covers.

Suddenly the kitten leaped out of the bed and quickly scampered out of the bedroom. "Come back, little kitty," called Diane. "Come sleep with me!"

Mother heard the noise and came to the door.

"Oh Mom," sobbed the heartbroken little girl. "My kitten won't stay in bed with me!"

Mother smiled and said, "God didn't mean for kittens to be held through the night while you sleep. Why don't you sleep with your favorite doll? Dolls love to sleep with children."

Sleep, my child, and peace attend thee,
    All through the night;
Guardian angels God will send thee,
    All through the night.

Soft and drowsy hours are creeping,
    Hill and vale in slumber sleeping,
I my loving vigil keeping,
    All through the night.

While the moon her watch is keeping,
    All through the night,
While the weary world is sleeping,
    All through the night.

O'er thy spirit gently stealing,
    Visions of delight revealing,
Breathes a pure and holy feeling,
    All through the night.

God, That Madest Earth and Heaven

God, that madest earth and heaven,
    Darkness and light;
Who the day for toil hast given,
    For rest the night;
May Thine angel-guards defend us,
    Slumber sweet Thy mercy send us,
Holy dreams and hopes attend us,
    This livelong night.

Who Can Count the Stars?

Mary and Catherine sat beside the window. It was time for bed, but Mother said they could say good night to the moon and stars.

"Good night, Moon and all the stars," said Mary as she looked out at the night sky.

"I can count the stars," Catherine bragged. "Two, three, four, fifteen, sixteen,..."

"No Catherine," Mary interrupted. "No one can count all the stars!"

"No one?"

"No one," Mary paused. "No one but God. God knows all the stars. God is so wonderful that He calls each star by name."

O Gladsome Light

O gladsome light, O grace
    Of God the Father's face,
The eternal splendor wearing;
    Celestial, holy, blest,
Our Savior Jesus Christ,
    Joyful in Thine appearing.

Now, before day fadeth quite,
    We see the evening light,
Our wonted hymn outpouring;
    Father of might unknown,
Thee, His incarnate Son,
    And Holy Spirit adoring.

Father, bless me in my body.
Father, bless me in my soul.
Father, bless me this night
in my body and my soul.

Jesus said:
"Do not worry about tomorrow,
for tomorrow will worry about itself. Each
day has enough trouble of its own."

Matthew 6:34

Now the Day Is Over

Now the day is over,
    Night is drawing nigh,
Shadows of the evening
    Steal across the sky.

Now the darkness gathers,
    Stars begin to peep,
Birds and beasts and flowers
    Soon will be asleep.

Jesus, give the weary
    Calm and sweet repose;
With Thy tender blessing
    May our eyelids close.

Now I lay me down to sleep.
I pray Thee, Lord, my soul to keep.
Your love be with me through the night
And wake me with the morning light.

Lord, keep us safe this night,
Secure from all our fears.
May angels guard us while we sleep,
Till morning light appears.

I'm Not Afraid Anymore!

"Mommy, please don't turn off the light," said Dan. "I'm afraid."

Dan saw dark shadows bouncing around his room. "The monsters will get me!"

Mother knew that Dan was afraid to go to sleep. As she closed the blinds, she said, "You know, things seem scary at times, but Jesus is always with you. Why don't we ask Jesus to protect you tonight. He will watch over you while you sleep. Let's pray."

After they prayed, Dan looked up at his mother. "I want to thank Jesus for helping me. I am not afraid of the dark when I know Jesus is with me."

Little Jesus, Sweetly Sleep, Do Not Stir

Little Jesus, sweetly sleep, do not stir,
    We will lend a coat of fur.
We will rock You, rock You, rock You,
    We will rock You, rock You, rock You:
See the fur to keep You warm,
    Snugly round Your tiny form.

Mary's little baby, sleep, sweetly sleep,
    Sleep in comfort, slumber deep.
We will rock You, rock You, rock You,
    We will rock You, rock You, rock You:
We will serve You all we can,
    Darling, darling little Man.

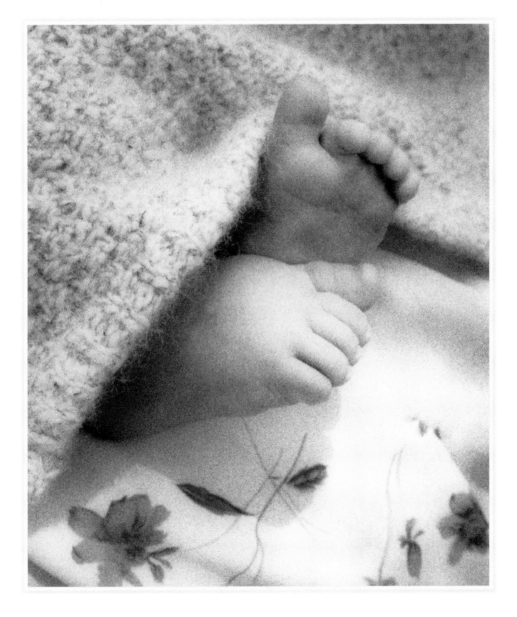

I see the moon.
　　The moon sees me.
God bless the moon,
　　And God bless me.

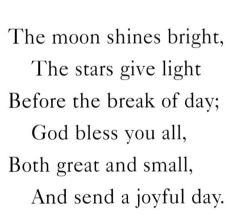

The moon shines bright,
　　The stars give light
Before the break of day;
　　God bless you all,
Both great and small,
　　And send a joyful day.

Sleep little one.
Mama is here to tuck
you into your cozy bed
and give you a kiss.
Have pleasant dreams
and know that Jesus and I
will be watching you
and keeping you safe
throughout the night.

Safely Through Another Week

Safely through another week
    God has brought us on our way.
Let us now a blessing seek,
    Waiting in His courts today:
Day of all the week the best,
    Emblem of eternal rest;
Day of all the week the best,
    Emblem of eternal rest.

Sleep Well

"It's time for bed, Casey," said Mother as she came into the bedroom to tuck in her daughter.

"Mommy, does Jesus really listen to my prayers?"

Mother looked at Casey's trusting face. "Yes, Casey, Jesus loves you and wants you to talk to Him."

"I'm sure other kids talk to Him, too. Maybe He's too busy to listen," said Casey.

"Jesus always has time to listen to a child's prayer."

Casey began to pray, "Dear Jesus, I love You. Thank you for Mommy and Daddy. Thank you for my house. Thank you for letting me play. Bless Teddy and help him not to be afraid in the dark."

Day Is Done

Day is done.
  Gone the sun
From the lakes,
  From the hills,
From the sky.

All is well.
  Safely rest,
God is nigh.

I will lie down and sleep in peace, for You alone,
O Lord, make me dwell in safety.

Psalm 4:8

Lord Jesus,
Sometimes at night I am scared.
I think I hear noises and see strange shadows.
Lord, help me to remember that You are with me
and that I need not be afraid.

Amen.

O God, make us children of quietness,
and heirs of peace.

St. Clement

Good night! Good night!
　　Far flies the light;
But still God's love
　　Shall flame above,
Making all bright.
　　Good night! Good night!

Victor Hugo